Everton

The Official
Everton
Football Club
Annual 2008

Written By Darren Griffiths, Scott McLeod,
Matthew Gamble & Claire Boden

A Grange Publication

© 2007. Published by Grange Communications Ltd., Edinburgh,
under licence from Everton Football Club. Printed in the EU.

ISBN 978-1-905426-82-9

£6.99

Contents

There's nothing like
Goodison when the fans
are making a tremendous
amount of noise.

THE MANAGER'S MATCH-DAY

David Moyes lives in Lancashire and so the drive to Goodison Park for home matches takes just under an hour...as long as the traffic is not too busy. He always makes sure that he leaves in plenty of time as he would much prefer to be early and have time to kill than be late and end up rushing.

However, no matter how early he is, there are always Everton supporters milling around Goodison when his car swings into the main car park. The boss always stops to sign autographs and have a quick chat about the game. His relationship with the Evertonians has been brilliant from the day he first arrived at the club in 2002.

It's about half-past twelve when he walks along the side of the pitch to make his way to the dressing-room area.

Once again, there are always people to chat to. The stewards are starting to get ready for their afternoon's work and they always shout across to wish him all the best and he often sees former Everton player, Graeme Sharp, showing some guests around the stadium. Sometimes he will bump into one of the television commentators such as John Motson or Martin Tyler and it's nice to catch-up with them, too.

More often than not, the team for the match is selected on the Friday afternoon but sometimes the odd player may need a fitness test on the day of the game before a decision is made on the final line-up.

The manager's match-day office is close to the home dressing room and it's where the boss and the coaches get changed. Some managers always wear suits but David tends to prefer to be in a tracksuit. The kitman knows exactly what he likes to wear and it's always laid out for him in his office when he arrives at the ground.

The kitman fills the official teamsheet in and Alan Irvine, the assistant manager, will hand it in to the referee one hour before the kick-off, which is the Premier League rule.

David always watches the entire match from the dug-out. Again, managers differ on this and some find it an advantage to watch the first-half from a seat in the stand. But the Blues boss likes to be close to the action and close enough to issue instructions to the players.

There's nothing like Goodison when the fans are making a tremendous amount of noise and the manager needs to shout to be heard during the game!

After the match, he will speak to the players as a group and then have a word with some of them individually, depending on how the game has gone.

Then there is the press to speak to. Accompanied by the club Press Officer, David does post-match interviews for TV, radio and written press. He may not always enjoy doing it but it's part and parcel of the game these days and has to be done.

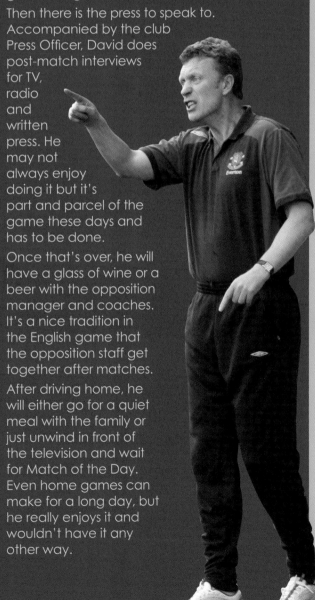

Once that's over, he will have a glass of wine or a beer with the opposition manager and coaches. It's a nice tradition in the English game that the opposition staff get together after matches.

After driving home, he will either go for a quiet meal with the family or just unwind in front of the television and wait for Match of the Day. Even home games can make for a long day, but he really enjoys it and wouldn't have it any other way.

evertonfc.com

This annual is full of loads of information – but to make sure you continue to keep up with all the latest from the Blues the best place for you is evertonfc.com.

Voted by fans as the number one website of any club in the Premiership at the end of 2006/07 season, evertonfc.com was made even better in the summer. Podcasts, blogs and the ability to leave your own comments on stories are just some of the elements that make it one of the most fan-friendly football sites around.

There are great games to keep you occupied – and quizzes to test your love of the Blues!

David Moyes talks to the website regularly and throughout the season there are webchats with members of the squad, giving you the opportunity to fire questions directly to the players who provide so much entertainment for fans every week.

There is an eBay-style auction section of the site that allows you to bid for all the latest signed merchandise and the EvertonMobile pages offer ringtones and screensavers that will make your phone the envy of all your Everton mates.

Exclusive match photography means you see all the best action shots of the players from each Premiership game – and if you want to you can even order copies of your favourite photographs.

Everything you could possibly need relating to Everton can be found at evertonfc.com – so pay it a visit today!

Alan Stubbs celebrates... despite the snow!

Season Review
part 1:

August

August began with a late friendly win over Aberdeen, and ended with Everton's first league win at Tottenham in 20 years.

In between was sandwiched a Howard Kendall testimonial, a home win over Watford and a 1-1 draw at Blackburn.

After Tim Cahill and Victor Anichebe had secured

Andy Johnson in action on his Everton Premiership debut

the win at Aberdeen, the Toffees slipped to a 1-0 reverse at the hands of Athletic Bilbao.

But the result was largely insignificant as fans and club officials paid tribute to the most successful manager in the club's history.

Then, on to serious Premiership business. Everton hosted Watford in the curtain raiser and were on their way when Andy Johnson netted his first strike for the Blues after just 14 minutes.

The eventual score was 2-1 after a late Watford worrier.

Tim Cahill came off the bench with a late leveler at Ewood Park before the Toffees made the trip to White Hart Lane a few days later.

Despite being reduced to ten men, Everton prevailed; Andy Johnson was again on the scoresheet in a 2-0 victory.

Everton celebrate scoring at Tottenham

September

This is a month that not only stands out in 2006's history; it stands out in Everton's entire club history.

And all because of one result. The first game of the month was the 204th Merseyside derby.

There were high hopes amongst the Goodison faithful, thanks to the promising start to the season and the arrival of hot prospects Joleon Lescott and Andy Johnson.

But even those expectations were put into the shade by the match itself.

Tim Cahill, a player with a great habit of netting against Everton's local rivals, did what he does best in the 24th minute - ghosting in, timing his run to perfection to punish a Liverpool defence that had failed to pick him up.

His cool finish under Pepe Reina was merely the pre-cursor however - the warm-up for the star of the show.

Johnson was that man - netting a cool finish in the opening period and a poacher's strike late in the game after an error by Reina.

The image of the hitman wheeling away after that final strike gesturing the 3-0 scoreline to the home fans is one that will live long in the memory.

And so whilst Everton remained unbeaten throughout the month of September, none of the four matches that followed that month came close to matching the derby for drama, entertainment and sheer passion.

Indeed, the next match proved something of a frustration - Everton leading twice against Wigan but being pegged back on both occasions by Paul Jewell's men.

A draw at Newcastle and another late equaliser from Manchester City in the final home game of the month ensured that, after the superb derby win, Everton ended the month ruing what should have been in terms of league position.

In the Carling Cup Victor Anichebe was given his first senior start as the Blues edged a second round tie at Peterborough 2-1.

Andy Johnson scores the 3rd goal against Liverpool

Tim Cahill scores the opener against Liverpool

October

After the highs of September, October 2006 was where things went a little awry for the Toffees.

It started badly, with the first defeat of the campaign in the shape of a 2-1 reverse at Middlesbrough.

Despite a creditable performance, goals from Mark Viduka and Yakubu put the Blues to the sword.

In the wake of dropped points at home against both Wigan and Manchester City, Everton boss David Moyes knew his side's decent league placing should have been so much better.

The response was positive. Penalties and Andy Johnson have not made happy bedfellows in 2006 - thanks to a series of controversial refereeing decisions which infuriated Everton's fans.

The suggestion in the media was that comments from rival managers about the player had influenced the judgement of match officials. If that was the case, then this was the game where the comments began.

Neil Warnock was not happy with the penalty that was awarded for a foul on Johnson by Claude Davis. And he made his feelings abundantly clear after a game Everton went on to win 2-0.

Although Everton were awarded four penalties in the Premiership between August and December, only one was for a foul on Johnson - and he was undoubtedly the most fouled Everton player in those months.

Nevertheless, following that victory a 4-0 thumping of Luton in the League Cup continued to boost the side's spirits. The most notable strike of that contest was a late Anichebe effort - his first of the season - underlining his growing credentials.

A 1-1 draw at Arsenal earned courtesy of the ubiquitous Tim Cahill's headed strike ensured the month ended well.

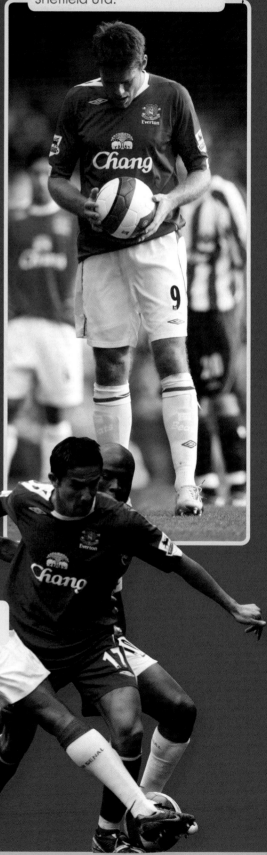

James Beattie gets ready to take his penalty against Sheffield Utd.

Goalscorer Tim Cahill battles for possession at Arsenal

November

November was a hectic month for the Blues. Six games were dealt with during the calendar month. Having drawn at The Emirates at the end of October, the second game of November was a League Cup clash with the Gunners at Goodison.

It was a younger, more inexperienced side fielded by Arsene Wenger. Everton had the upper hand but a late Emanuel Adebayor goal from a corner put paid to Everton's hopes - and ruled out the prospect of extra time.

It was a soft goal to concede, rubbing salt into Everton's wounds having played the better of the two sides.

It came just days after a 1-0 reverse at Fulham's Craven Cottage in which Andy Johnson was denied a great penalty claim that would have provided the Blues with an opportunity to secure a share of the spoils.

A hat-trick of 1-0 defeats was completed by a home reverse to Aston Villa.

Veteran striker Chris Sutton netted the only goal of the game minutes before the interval. The late appearance of Anichebe was the silver lining for the Blues, with the young hitman once again demonstrating why he is a hot property.

Everton got back to winning ways - and back on the scoring trail - with a 1-0 victory over Bolton.

With Johnson having not netted since September and Cahill ruled out until the New Year following a freak collision with Lee Carsley against Villa, it was Mikel Arteta who took the goalscoring baton.

His sublime solo-strike is one of the highlights of 2006. Ironic, then, that it came in such a low-key encounter.

A week later and an own goal gave Everton the upper-hand at Charlton before Andy Reid equalised late on with a fierce strike for the relegation threatened outfit.

Next up it was Manchester United at Old Trafford where a 3-0 defeat ensured a dismal end to November.

The stats for the month did not make the best reading - four defeats, one victory and a draw.

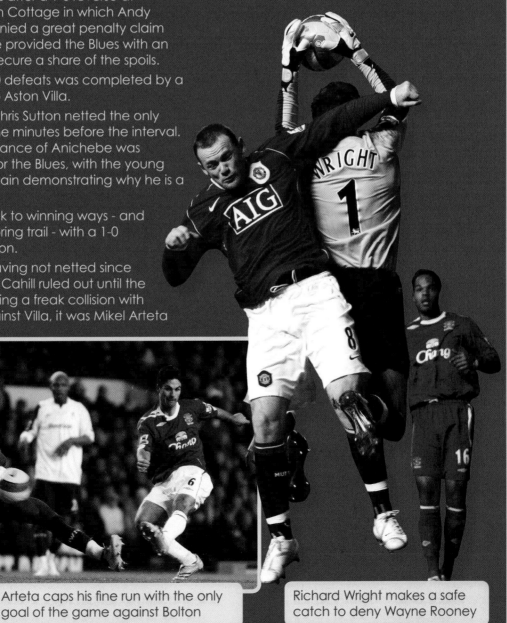

Arteta caps his fine run with the only goal of the game against Bolton

Richard Wright makes a safe catch to deny Wayne Rooney

December

Having persevered through November despite a spate of injuries, things slowly began to improve in terms of numbers in December.

And that return of players was reflected in improved results.

A decent 2-0 win and home performance against West Ham started the month on the day the Blues were drawn against Blackburn in the third round of the FA Cup.

The goals against Alan Pardew's men were netted by Leon Osman - his first of the campaign and what a fine goal - and James Vaughan.

It wasn't just the young striker's first of the season, it was his first senior goal for 18 months, ending a nightmare spell with injuries.

With Vaughan and Anichebe snapping at the heels of experienced forwards such as Andy Johnson, James Beattie and James McFadden the club's goalscoring prospects look good.

That decent result was followed by a poor performance, a succession of enforced tactical changes and a 2-0 reverse at Portsmouth - the club's first Premiership defeat at Fratton Park.

The response? A superb display against Chelsea as Arteta, Osman and Neville returned to fitness following injury.

An Arteta penalty and a powerful Joseph Yobo header gave Everton a 2-1 lead entering the final 10 minutes of the match. But super strikes from Frank Lampard and Didier Drogba broke Everton hearts.

Lesser sides may have buckled in their next performance - the Toffees didn't. Reading were swept aside two days before

James McFadden scores against Reading

Christmas at The Madejski Stadium.

Andy Johnson's return to scoring form and a good strike from James McFadden sealed the three points - Everton's first away win since the August success at Tottenham.

That win should have been followed by another on Boxing Day but Middlesbrough's defensive approach frustrated the home side.

Another penalty claim was ignored and a goalless draw followed.

Having started 2006 with a victory at Goodison, the year ended with one as well. Victor Anichebe netted twice and Phil Neville grabbed his first ever Everton goal to ensure Newcastle were brushed aside 3-0.

Victor Anichebe nets his second goal against Newcastle

Joseph Yobo heads home against Chelsea

Tim Cahill celebrates his equaliser at Newcastle United

Joleon Lescott scores against Charlton Athletic

James McFadden scores
Everton's Goal of the Season
against Charlton Athletic…

… and wheels away in celebration

Phil Jagielka

- Phil Jagielka joined Everton in the summer of 2007 from Sheffield United.

- He arrived on Merseyside in early July in a deal worth £4m.

- Rumours of a switch to Goodison Park had rumbled on all summer, and when Sheffield United's relegation was confirmed (following their challenge of the Premier League's decision not to dock West Ham points) the Toffees quickly tied up the deal.

- Jagielka, who has England 'B' honours, is a versatile player.

- He can play in central defence, at full back and also in midfield.

- He is also a capable goalkeeper and was called into action for Sheffield United on several occasions, most notably when he kept a clean sheet in the Blades' 1-0 home win over Arsenal last season.

- Jagielka was at Everton's academy for a period in his teens before progressing through the ranks at the Yorkshire side.

Everton Quiz

1 Who were Everton's opponents for the first game of this season?

2 From what team did Everton sign Phil Jagielka?

3 What squad number is Phil Neville?

4 Which of Everton's strikers has played for Birmingham and Crystal Palace?

5 Who is wearing the number 5 shirt for Everton this season?

6 How many times have Everton won the FA cup?

7 Howard Kendall was manager of Everton how many times - 1, 2 or 3?

8 What is the name of Everton's old training ground?

9 In the 1927/28 season, how many league goals did Dixie Dean score for Everton?

10 Which international team does Tim Cahill play for?

11 Which Everton player became the Premiership's youngest ever goal scorer in the season 04/05?

12 Everton were founded in which year?

13 Who scored for Everton in the 1995 FA Cup win against Manchester United?

14 Everton lost to whom to knock them out of the Champions League in 2005?

15 True or False? Everton have been in top-flight football longer than any other club.

Answers on page 62

Picture Quiz

Answers on page 62

James Vaughan is celebrating a goal against which club?

1

2

Who is the player under the pile of bodies?

AJ is celebrating after scoring against Arsenal, but who was in goal for the Gunners?

3

Joleon Lescott is celebrating at which Premier League ground?

5

What shirt number is Victor Anichebe wearing in this photo?

4

List the three international players in the pic?

7

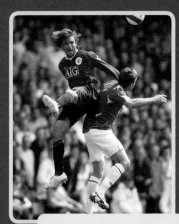

Against which teams did James Beattie score last season?

6

Who is the Bolton player obscured by Leon Osman?

8

21

2006/07 Statistics

Premiership

Date	Opponent	Result	Scorers	Att
Sat 19 Aug	Watford (H)	2-1	Johnson, Arteta	39,691
Wed 23 Aug	Blackburn (A)	1-1	Cahill	22,015
Sat 26 Aug	Tottenham H (A)	2-0	Davenport og, Johnson	35,540
Sat 9 Sep	Liverpool (H)	3-0	Johnson 2, Cahill	40,004
Sat 16 Sep	Wigan (H)	2-2	Johnson, Beattie	37,117
Sun 24 Sep	Newcastle (A)	1-1	Cahill	50,107
Sat 30 Sep	Man City (H)	1-1	Johnson	38,250
Sat 14 Oct	Middlesbrough (A)	1-2	Cahill	27,156
Sat 21 Oct	Sheffield Utd (H)	2-0	Arteta, Beattie	37,900
Sat 28 Oct	Arsenal (A)	1-1	Cahill	60,047
Sat 4 Nov	Fulham (A)	0-1	-	23,327
Sat 11 Nov	Aston Villa (H)	0-1	-	36,376
Sat 18 Nov	Bolton W (H)	1-0	Arteta	34,417
Sat 25 Nov	Charlton A (A)	1-1	Hreidarsson og	26,453
Wed 29 Nov	Manchester Utd (A)	0-3	-	75,723
Sun 3 Dec	West Ham (H)	2-0	Vaughan, Osman	32,968
Sat 9 Dec	Portsmouth (A)	0-2		19,258
Sun 17 Dec	Chelsea (H)	2-3	Yobo, Arteta	33,970
Sat 23 Dec	Reading (A)	2-0	McFadden, Johnson	24,053
Tues 26 Dec	Middlesbrough (H)	0-0	-	38,126
Sat 30 Dec	Newcastle (H)	3-0	Neville, Anichebe 2	38,682
Mon 1 Jan	Man City (A)	1-2	Osman	39, 836
Sun 14 Jan	Reading (H)	1-1	Johnson	34,772
Sun 21 Jan	Wigan (A)	2-0	Arteta 2	18,149
Sat 3 Feb	Liverpool (A)	0-0	-	44,234
Sat 10 Feb	Blackburn (H)	1-0	Johnson	35,593
Wed 21 Feb	Tottenham H (H)	1-2	Arteta	34,121
Sat 24 Feb	Watford (A)	3-0	Fernandes, Johnson, Osman,	18,761
Sat 3 Mar	Sheffield Utd (A)	1-1	Arteta	32,019
Sun 18 Mar	Arsenal (H)	1-0	Johnson	37,162
Mon 2 Apr	Aston Villa (A)	1-1	Lescott	36,407
Fri 6 Apr	Fulham (H)	4-1	Stubbs, Carsley, Vaughan, Anichebe	5,612
Mon 9 Apr	Bolton W (A)	1-1	Vaughan	25,179
Sun 15 Apr	Charlton A (H)	2-1	Lescott, McFadden	34,028
Sat 21 Apr	West Ham (A)	0-1	-	34,945
Sat 28 Apr	Manchester Utd (H)	2-4	Stubbs, Fernandes	39,682
Sat 5 May	Portsmouth (H)	3-0	Arteta, Yobo, Naysmith	39, 619
Sun 13 May	Chelsea (A)	1-1	Vaughan	41,746

FA Cup

Date	Opponent	Result	Scorers	Att
Sun 7 Jan	Blackburn R (H)	1-4	Johnson	24,246

Carling Cup

Date	Opponent	Result	Scorers	Att
Tues 19 Sept	Peterborough U (A)	2-1	Stirling og Cahill	10,756
Tues 24 Oct	Luton Town (H)	4-0	Cahill, Keane og, McFadden, Anichebe	27,129
Wed 8 Nov	Arsenal (H)	0-1	-	31,045

Everton Ladies Manager
Mo Marley

EVERTON LADIES

2007/08 marks a venture into the unknown for Everton Ladies. A place in the UEFA Cup for the first time in the club's history beckons.

The Toffees finished second in the FA Women's Premier League behind the all-conquering Arsenal team but as The Gunners also won this season's UEFA Cup competition it meant that an extra place went to an English club for the next campaign.

The Blues enjoyed a sensational start to the 2006/07 season. Fresh from a pre-season tour of Canada – the first in the club's history - Mo Marley's side went four games unbeaten and notched an impressive 2-1 victory against Charlton Athletic on the opening day of the season.

A defeat to Doncaster Rovers Belles halted the run in mid September and a 4-1 loss to Arsenal in October 2006 underlined the dominance of The Gunners, who were still unbeaten.

Injuries to a number of key senior players notably Fern Whelan dented Everton's quest for top spot and a number of indifferent results towards the end of 2006 left the Toffees further adrift of Arsenal.

The turn of the year marked a change in fortunes and Everton started 2007 with a comprehensive 6-0 victory over Millwall in the FA Cup. However the cup run came to an end against old foes Charlton in the third round.

With Arsenal running away with the league, the battle for second place was a straight race between the Blues and Charlton. An eight match unbeaten run secured the runners-up spot for Mo Marley's side and a 9-0 win against Fulham was one of the high points of the season.

Everton finished two points ahead of the Addicks and 14 points adrift of the irrepressible Gunners, who won every competitive fixture played in 2006/07.

Having achieved a second place finish for the past two consecutive seasons, there is plenty of room for optimism for the Toffees in bridging the distance between Arsenal and the chasing pack.

Goalkeeper Rachel Brown is the current England number one and is touted as one of the best shot-stoppers in the women's game. Brown is an integral part of the Three Lions side and helped England achieve qualification for the World Cup in 2007.

Everton can also boast one of the best known faces in the women's game: Rachel Unitt. A powerful defender with a sweet left foot, Rachel's performances for both club and country resulted in her being named England Women's Player of the Year in 2006.

The club's longest serving player Kelly McDougall is an integral part of the team and her consistent performances in the heart of midfield earned international honours for the Toffees' vice-captain.

The future is certainly looking bright with a number of the younger members of the squad earning recognition with England Under-19s. Danielle Hill, Fern Whelan and Faye McCoy are the names to look out for in the coming years.

Everton have an inspirational leader in the figure of Mo Marley. Marley is one of the most respected people in the women's game and when not guiding the Toffees, she spends her time with England coaching at various levels, notably the Under-19s.

LEIGHTON BAINES

When Leighton Baines signed for Everton just a few days before the start of the season, he knew he had made the right move in returning to the Club he supports.

The Toffees moved to sign one of the brightest defensive prospects in England when they signed Baines in the summer.

Baines arrived at Goodison Park from Wigan Athletic, where he had earned a reputation as a high quality attacking left back.

He also played regularly for England Under-21s, and to cap it off, Leighton and his family are Everton supporters.

He was even in the Blues' academy for a while in his teens before joining Wigan and eventually racking up nearly 150 appearances for the Lancashire side.

Other top sides were interested in signing him, but the young left-back was quick to confirm that there was only one team he really wanted to join.

"Obviously it was the place people knew I wanted to come," said Leighton. "There were other things happening and I started to wonder will it happen or won't it, but I was happy when it was all done.

"It is great to be here. I am a local lad and a lot of my family support Everton so it's good to be here at last."

When he was playing for the Under-21s, Leighton met up with Everton striker James Vaughan and the two have become good friends.

"I got to know Vaughany well over the summer," explained Leighton. "We spent a lot of time together and I spend a bit of time with him now when we can, if we have got a bit of spare time!"

Baines believes that there is plenty of potential for exciting times at Everton, with David Moyes having assembled an ambitious, multi-talented squad.

"There seems to be a good mix here," continued the fullback. "There are some experienced lads and quite a few good young lads as well - Vaughany being one of them - and people like Victor Anichebe as well. Those two look like a handful up front and playing against them two last season wasn't easy."

International Blues...

Joseph Yobo

Lee Carsley

Tim Howard

Nuno Valente

Which country do these international stars play for?

Write your answer underneath the picture and turn to page 62 to see if you are correct...

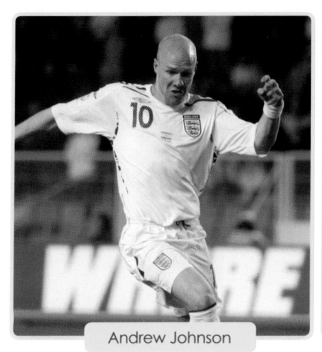

Andrew Johnson

James McFadden

Tim Cahill

Andy van der Meyde

29

Everton in USA

USA keeper Tim Howard at full stretch in his home country.

Tony Hibbert stays focussed on the ball during a session in Salt Lake City.

Leon Osman plays the ball forward during the game against Real Salt Lake

James Beattie is on the receiving end of a strong aerial challenge.

The squad warm-up in the baking sunlight Stateside.

Phil Neville emerges with the ball during a training game.

Phil Jagielka at full stretch against the MLS side.

Star man Mikel Arteta holds off the attention of the Salt Lake defender.

Typical Training Day

A typical training day for the Everton players can begin very early.

Although training sessions at the Club's new base at Finch Farm on the outskirts of the city get underway at 10.30am, manager David Moyes asks all his players to report in by 10am. And for some of the players who live a long distance away that can mean an early start.

That is why so many of the players live within an hour's drive of the training ground. In fact, the players who live close together share lifts to make sure they all arrive together and on time.

Most arrive before 9.30am to make the most of the breakfast on offer in the great canteen. As the lads read through the papers, Everton assistant boss Alan Irvine and the manager go out onto the training pitch with first-team coach Jimmy Lumsden to prepare for the forthcoming session. That could mean positioning cones and markers out in keeping with the training routines that are planned.

The players will go through their paces on the training ground, following the intricate instructions of the coaches, for up to two hours. If it is the day before a game this work will focus on specific tactics and set-piece work.

After returning to the dressing room and having a shower the players will return to the canteen for lunch. The manager could then make use of the state-of-the-art video lounge within the training ground in order to go through specific tactics or to look at videos of the opposition.

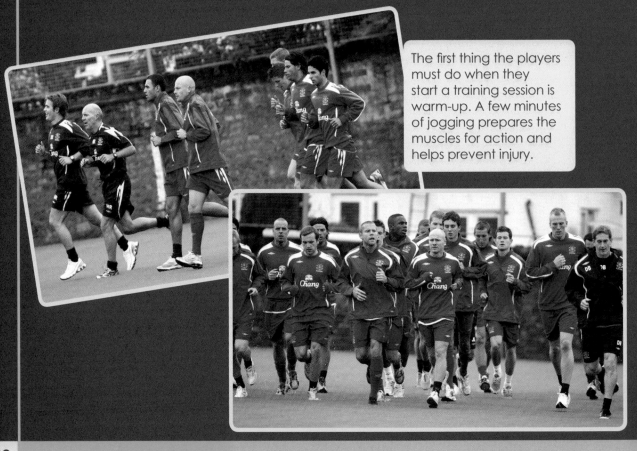

The first thing the players must do when they start a training session is warm-up. A few minutes of jogging prepares the muscles for action and helps prevent injury.

Next up it's time for some all important stretching exercises to warm the muscles further and get them ready for more strenuous activities.

The players are always delighted when they get a touch of the ball, and these exercises help improve the touch and passing skills.

There's no respite for the goalkeepers! They split up from the rest of the players after the warm up and goalkeeping coach Chris Woods puts them through their paces with some special drills.

Meanwhile, Blues assistant boss Alan Irvine splits the players into two sides for some game-type practices.

Even though it's a training session, the Everton boys always give 100 per cent and there's a healthy competitive spirit throughout the squad.

After the session David Moyes gives his feedback and offers some coaching points to the players.

ANDY JOHNSON

I started kicking a football around almost as soon as I could walk and the biggest enjoyment I have always got from the game has been scoring goals.

Even if I was just whacking a ball about in the street or in the local park with my pals as a youngster, I just wanted to score goals.

Whenever I watched Match of the Day or if I went to an actual game I would always keep a close eye on the centre-forwards and then try to copy what they did in the school playground.

I am lucky that I have always been a fast runner. At school I was one of the fastest and that was a great asset for me to have in the football team.

But, of course, even if you have all the pace in the world you still need to put the ball into the net when you get the opportunity and I used to practice all the time.

Like most young boys, most of my spare time was spent playing football and even if I was on my own I used to pretend that I was playing in a cup final and I would score the winning goal!

I'd spend hours kicking against a goal chalked onto a wall and I would place the ball to the right of the goal, the left of the goal and even try to hit the 'bar'. It was all good practice for when I actually played in games.

You can never have too much practice and although the one thing you cannot really prepare for is the pressure of being through on goal in front of 40,000 people, you can still always work on technique and accuracy.

All those hours belting a ball on my own certainly stood me in good stead as I grew older.

My heroes when I was at school were players like Gary Lineker and Ian Wright. I had every respect for the types who made goalscoring look easy. The very best goal-getters are absolute naturals and Lineker and Wright were amongst the finest in the world at their peak.

Even now I still have a huge admiration for the likes of Didier Drogba and Thierry Henry – players who can regularly hit something like 20 goals in a Premier League season.

I always set myself a target at the start of each season but I never reveal the figure and I never tell anyone whether or not I have reached it.

What I will say is that one of my ambitions when I joined Everton was to score in a Merseyside derby and so to find the net twice in a 3-0 win in my first derby was unbelievable!

The thrill of scoring a goal is unique but to do it in the white-hot atmosphere of a Merseyside derby really was something special.

It was a dream come true for me... and that schoolboy cup final dream is still waiting for me too!

Spot the Difference
Can you find all 6 differences?
Turn to page 62 to find the answers...

Everton celebrate a James Vaughan goal

It's an exciting time at Everton's academy!

After producing a host of Premiership stars at the old training base in the Netherton area of Liverpool, the next generation of Everton stars are now training at the new Finch Farm training ground.

The new facility has the very best of everything and it means the young players can rub shoulders with the Toffees' current Premier League players.

The most recent players to move up from the academy to the first team are Victor Anichebe and James Vaughan, and the likes of Leon Osman and Tony Hibbert are now experienced pros after coming through the ranks.

Players such as Patrick Boyle and Bjarni Vidarsson have also trained at the academy and they could well be the next players to break through into the first team setup.

In fact, the latest academy intake hoping to make the grade was of such a quality that academy director Ray Hall had to bend the rules to get them all on board!

"We have actually got more than we usually take on because of the quality," said Ray. "We are taking 11 boys on and we feel we have got as good a group coming into us as we have had for many years."

Ray admits he couldn't wait to move in to the state-of-the-art new training facility.

Academy Player of the Year Shaun Densmore

"Everyone was tremendously excited by the move," explained Ray.

"I can see this really benefiting the young players. They will have the chance to observe how top professionals go about their daily business. We all learn by looking at good examples. We have tried to make the integration and transition as seamless as possible.

"From being on two different sites to being within 100 yards of each other is a tremendous opportunity. We want to help develop more players for the manager to have at his disposal."

Ray and his team work extremely hard all year round as they try to attract and train the very best young players for David Moyes to take advantage of.

"The ambition of this football club is to get back into the top four and we - the Academy - have to give the manager as much help as possible. We are part of that process," he continued.

"I'm selfish, in that I would like to see a few more but I'm also sure the manager wants to see a few more youngsters coming through too.

"We have a system here that we have worked hard at developing. There are a lot of good people here who want the kids to succeed.

"The competition we have to attract kids here is enormous. On our doorstep we have one of the biggest football clubs in the world in Manchester United, so we have to work very hard in that once a young boy comes to Everton, we have to keep them.

"Obviously the dream is to have 11 Scousers on the pitch and wouldn't that be great?"

"...the feeling of pride that I feel whenever I pull any sort of top over my head that includes the 'Three Lions' will never subside."

One of the greatest thrills that a footballer can experience is playing for his country and I have been very fortunate to have represented England more than fifty times.

I was still only 19 when I was first selected to play for England and I will never forget the feeling of pride and excitement I felt when Sir Alex Ferguson told me of my inclusion when I was training at Manchester United.

Of course, I was absolutely delighted for myself but I was also overjoyed at the thought of just how proud my family would be.

My mum and dad have supported me every step of the way through junior football right through to the professional ranks and I know it was a hugely proud day for them when I first played for England.

Their pride is doubled, of course, whenever my brother and I are in the same international line-up.

Very few brothers get to play in the same England team – Bobby and Jackie Charlton are the most famous – and so it was great for Gary and me to achieve it.

Invariably, international squads get together after the weekend games. If we're playing a home game at Wembley, we'll all meet up at a hotel base in the London area and it's always great to meet up with the lads again.

Being a part of the England set-up for so long has helped me to make many good friends and I was especially pleased at the back end of last season when my old pal David Beckham was recalled to the international fold.

When we arrive at the hotel we are given all our training gear and tracksuits and the feeling of pride that I

feel whenever I pull any sort of top over my head that includes the 'Three Lions' will never subside.

International training is different to club training because the FA allow the press in to watch the first half an hour or so.

There is always immense media interest in every England game and I myself have often sat alongside the manager at a press conference.

I have been lucky enough to play for five England managers and I have learned from each one of them – Terry Venables, Glenn Hoddle, Kevin Keegan, Sven Goran Eriksson and Steve McClaren.

I have played for my country in many different countries around the world and, of course, at many venues in this country while Wembley was being re-built.

But there is no doubt that playing at Wembley itself is the best.

Walking out onto that hallowed turf and standing in line in front of the Royal Box when the national anthem is played still makes the hairs on the back of my neck stand up.

It's an indescribable feeling and it's impossible not to think about all the famous English footballers who have done the same thing down the years.

I hope it's an experience that I will have again many times in the future...

Neville –
Playing for England

Player Profiles

Anderson Silva de Franca

Anderson de Silva first 'signed' for the Blues late in 2005.

But having reached agreement with Uruguayan club Montevideo over the player, Everton were unable to complete the Brazilian's registration because of immigration issues.

Everton renewed their interest in the player in January 2007 and signed him on a six month contract after finally securing a European passport.

Anderson made just one substitute appearance during the 2006/07 season but it was enough to earn a 12-month contract extension at Goodison.

Alan Stubbs

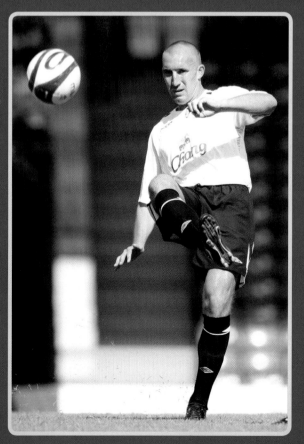

Alan Stubbs was released by Everton as a teenager but is now in his second stint at the club, after rejoining in January 2006.

His second move to Goodison followed a short spell at Sunderland at the start of the 2005/6 season.

Alan was brought in to boost a depleted backline; he can produce displays of the highest quality and is renowned for his ability to spray accurate passes all over the field.

His ability to strike a ball powerfully and accurately from distance has made him somewhat of a free-kick specialist.

Alan was a lynchpin of the side during 2006/07, with outstanding performances against the likes of Liverpool and Arsenal forcing David Moyes to switch Joleon Lescott to left back to accommodate both defenders. Stubbs' experience was invaluable in securing a UEFA Cup spot.

Andrew Johnson

Andrew Johnson became Everton's record signing when he joined from Crystal Palace for £8.6m in the summer of 2006.

He began his career at Birmingham City before joining Crystal Palace in 2002 as the makeweight in a transfer deal for Clinton Morrison, taking the value of £750,000 for the purposes of the transaction.

He finished the 2003/04 season as the top scorer in the First Division with 32 goals, helping Palace to promotion to the Premiership but better things were on the horizon... In the 2004/05 season he was the top English goalscorer in the Premiership and earned his first England cap in February 2005.

Despite his contribution of 21 goals the Eagles were relegated.

Everton fought off interest from both Wigan and Bolton in order to secure the striker's services for a fee of £8.6m.

He was a hit with Evertonians from day one, scoring six goals in his opening seven league matches including a brace in a famous 3-0 victory over Liverpool. He went on to finish as top scorer with 11 goals.

Andy van der Meyde

Andy van der Meyde became Everton's eighth signing of a hectic summer in 2005 when he arrived from Inter on transfer deadline day.

A talented winger capable of playing on either flank or as a second striker, he provided David Moyes with a wealth of further attacking options.

Andy began his career with his hometown club of Vitesse Arnhem in the Dutch top flight.

But his talents were quickly spotted by the mighty Ajax, who signed him in 1997 at the age of 17.

Between 2000 and 2003 the attacking winger made 86 senior appearances for Ajax, scoring 20 goals.

It was that form which attracted the attentions of Inter, with coach Hector Cuper snapping up Andy in the summer of 2003 in a £5m deal.

His pace and ability to deliver quality crosses from wide-positions are rated as his real assets.

After appearing 31 times for Inter, Andy was snapped up by David Moyes but his move to Goodison has been marred by injury and he has only managed a limited number of appearances since his arrival from Italy.

Bjarni Vidarsson

Bjarni was identified by the Blues' scouting network and has since moved up through the ranks at Goodison Park.

A tall, elegant midfielder, he enjoyed a fine season in the reserves last term, scoring four goals in his nine starts.

Subsequently his form impressed David Moyes enough for him to hand Bjarni a place on the subs bench for the matches against Newcastle in February and Middlesbrough in April.

Bjarni has represented his native Iceland at under-16, -17, -19 and -21 levels.

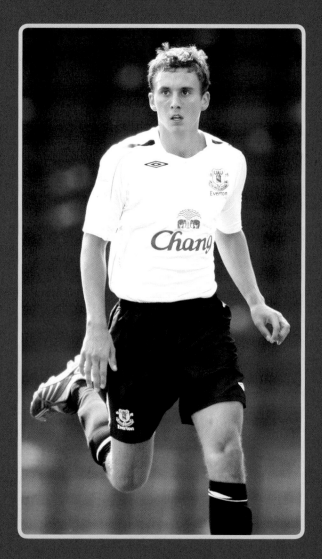

Iain Turner

Highly rated young goalkeeper Iain Turner arrived at Goodison in January 2003 in a £50,000 deal from Stirling Albion.

David Moyes swooped to sign Iain after he did well during a three-day trial.

He has impressed since arriving at Everton and made his debut as a late replacement for the injured Richard Wright in a 4-1 FA Cup fourth round defeat to Chelsea at Stamford Bridge in February 2006.

His Premiership debut came just three days later at Goodison against Blackburn but the young Scot lasted only eight minutes before being red-carded for handling the ball outside the penalty area.

In the Spring of 2007 Iain moved to Sheffield Wednesday on loan and it proved a hugely successful move. He remained unbeaten during his 11 game spell with The Owls.

James McFadden

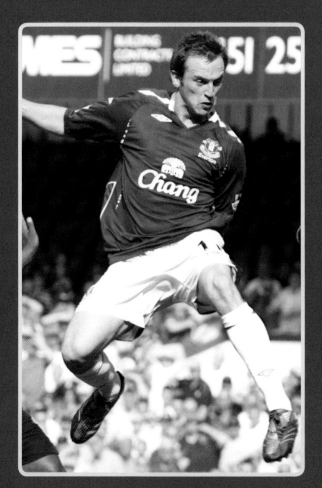

David Moyes beat off competition from Celtic, Rangers and Preston to secure the services of the Motherwell striker in a £1.25m deal in September 2003.

The Glasgow-born player worked his way up through the ranks at Fir Park and became a regular in the Motherwell first team and the Scotland squad by the age of 20.

His appearance as a substitute against South Africa in May 2002, earned him his first international cap, at the age of 19.

James can operate on either wing or in attack and he has scored a number of important goals for both Everton and Scotland.

The 2005/06 season was McFadden's best in an Everton shirt. He forged a good partnership with James Beattie, scoring some spectacular efforts in his haul of seven goals.

Injuries including a broken foot marred the following campaign but his wonder goal against Charlton Athletic in April 2007 was voted the Club's Goal of the Season.

James Vaughan

James joined Everton's Academy programme at nine years of age and scored a number of goals for the reserve team during the 2004/05 season, catching the eye of the manager.

Vaughan's 73rd minute substitute appearance against Crystal Palace on 10th April 2005 ensured that the 16-year-old from Birmingham broke Joe Royle's record as the Club's youngest first-team player by 11 days, as he was just 16 years and 271 days old!

Then his 84th minute strike not only made him Everton's youngest-ever scorer, surpassing Wayne Rooney at 16 years 360 days, but he also overtook James Milner as the Premiership's youngest scorer, who previously held the record at 16 years 357 days.

But early in the 2005/06 campaign he sustained a knee ligament injury whilst on international duty with England Under-18s. A series of complications meant the young striker was sidelined for the remainder of the campaign.

He returned to the first-team frame in 2006/07 and netted three times in six games at the end of the season. At the Club's End of Season Awards, James scooped the Young Player of the Season Award.

Vaughan's meteoric rise was accelerated when he made his England Under-21 debut against Italy at the European Under-21 Championships in June 2007.

Joseph Yobo

Joseph joined the Blues, declining offers from Arsenal and Juventus, to become David Moyes' first signing in the summer of 2002.

Joseph signed a 12-month contract with the Blues, with an option for a further four years, which was taken up by Moyes in November 2002.

Joseph's pace and versatility were major factors in his switch from the French giants as the Blues boss sought to bring the best young talent to Goodison.

His composure both on the ball and when under pressure belied his tender years. Good in the air, strong in the tackle and difficult to hassle off the ball, the defender also possesses tremendous vision - attributes which helped him earn Everton's Young Player of the Year Award for the 2003/04 season.

Joseph went on to play every second of every Premiership game during the 2006/07 season, matching a record last achieved 20 years earlier by Kevin Ratcliffe.

Joleon Lescott

Joleon Lescott signed for Everton in June 2006, joining from Championship side Wolves for an undisclosed fee.

The Birmingham-born player ended his Molineux career with 224 appearances and 13 goals to his name.

An instant hit at Goodison, Joleon played in every match of the 2006/07 season, won the Players' Player of the Year accolade and was called up to the England 'B' international squad by Steve McClaren at the end of the campaign.

Joleon played much of his first season out of position at left-back rather than his preferred position in the centre of defence.

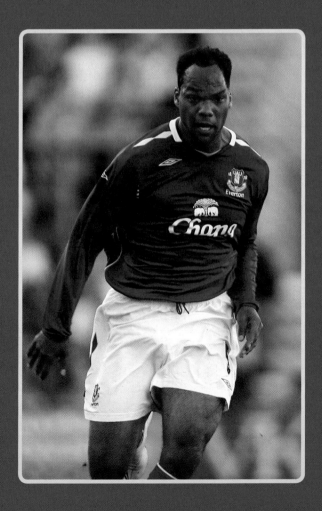

John Ruddy

John joined Everton in the summer of 2005, for a fee of £250,000.

He had impressed at his previous club, Cambridge United, making 39 appearances in League Two despite being only 18 when he made his professional debut.

He joined an impressive goalkeeping ranks at Everton, that included England internationals Nigel Martyn and Richard Wright.

He soon went out on loan to then-League One outfit Walsall and also completed a loan spell at Chester that same season.

John returned to Everton and made his debut in February in unusual circumstances.

Third choice keeper Iain Turner started the game against Blackburn, deputising for the injured Richard Wright and Nigel Martyn.

Turner was dismissed after just eight minutes for deliberate handball and John was thrust into the fray.

He managed to keep a clean sheet in a 1-0 Everton victory.

At the start of the 2006/07 season John enjoyed a successful loan spell at Stockport County and also made appearances for Wrexham and Bristol City, picking up vital experience along the way.

Leighton Baines

Leighton Baines joined Everton just a few days before the start of the season.

Recruited from Wigan, Baines became the third major signing of the summer following Phil Jagielka and Steven Pienaar.

Having been on the Toffees' books as a teenager, Baines eventually joined Wigan's youth scheme, making his senior debut at the age of 17.

He went on to make nearly 150 appearances for the Latics, impressing in the Premier League and becoming a regular for England Under-21s.

An attacking and tenacious left-back, Baines was a vital player for both his club and country, playing all England's games in the 2007 Euro Under-21 Championships.

Whilst on duty with the England squad Baines became friends with Everton's James Vaughan, and was soon able to link up with him on a regular basis after signing a five year deal with the Blues.

Lee Carsley

One of Walter Smith's final signings, the Republic of Ireland international has proved to be a lynchpin in David Moyes' senior squad.

Signed from Coventry in February, 2002 for £1.9m, Lee's whole-hearted approach to life in the midfield engine room has made him a valuable member of the senior squad.

Lee's career began with Derby, where he emerged through the youth ranks to make his debut in 1992 before going on to play for the Rams 166 times during almost a decade in the Midlands.

That form led to a move to Blackburn for £3.4m in March 1999 but within months of his arrival at Ewood Park Lee suffered the disappointment of relegation.

After just 21 months with Rovers, he was on his way again - this time to Coventry City for £2m.

Once again, relegation beckoned and it was midway through the following season that the Blues rescued Lee from the first division.

He has now played more than 100 times for Everton and was a key figure in securing a top six finish last term.

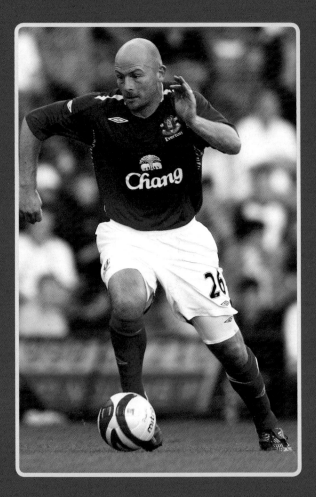

Leon Osman

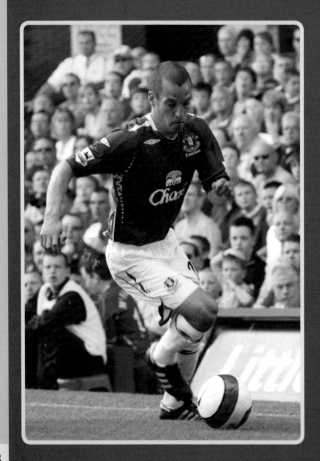

Leon Osman came through the ranks at Everton but his dreams of becoming a professional footballer were almost shattered in 2001 when he suffered a serious knee injury.

That injury kept him out of action for almost a year, but he has bounced back in style.

A midfielder who combines excellent passing and vision with an eye for goal, he forced his way into David Moyes' first-team plans with loan spells at Carlisle United and most notably at Derby County where he put in some delightful displays, scoring three goals in 17 appearances.

Following his spell at Pride Park, he went from strength to strength and was rewarded with a taste of senior action towards the end of the 2003/04 season scoring within five minutes of his full debut against Wolves at Molineux.

Leon became a first-team regular during the 2004/05 season and he followed that up with a strong showing in the 2005/6 season, scoring four goals and being one of Everton's most consistent performers in the latter part of the campaign.

Leon consolidated his position in 2006/07, making 37 appearances and netting three goals.

Lukas Jutkiewicz

Lukas Jutkiewicz arrived at Everton in the summer of 2007.

He agreed a deal in March of that year after emerging as one of the hottest young prospects in the lower divisions whilst at Swindon Town.

He helped the Robins to promotion back to League One at the end of the 2006/07 campaign before heading for the Premiership.

Lukas made his senior bow for Swindon in April 2006 when he was just 17.

He then switched to Everton in the close season and is certainly one for the future.

Mikel Arteta

The skilful central midfielder began his career with Barcelona at the age of 15 before moving to Paris Saint-Germain FC in 2000.

Glasgow Rangers bought him two years later for a fee of £5.8m and he was part of the team that won the Scottish Premier League, Scottish Cup and Scottish League Cup in 2003.

Real Sociedad paid £2.5m to take the player back to Spain, however Mikel struggled to hold down a regular place at La Real which prompted the Blues to sign him on loan in January 2005 until the end of the season with a view to a permanent move.

The playmaker impressed with a host of dazzling displays, including an eye-catching goal from a free-kick in the 4-0 defeat of Crystal Palace.

As a result of his form, the Blues chose to take up the option of signing him, concluding the deal in July 2005 for a fee of £2m.

The following two seasons Arteta was an essential part of Everton's attacking play which earned the Spaniard Everton Player of the Year two seasons running.

Mikel was ranked by the ACTIM Index as the sixth best player in the Premiership for the 2006/07 season. During the summer of 2007 he signed a five-year contract extending his stay at Goodison until 2012.

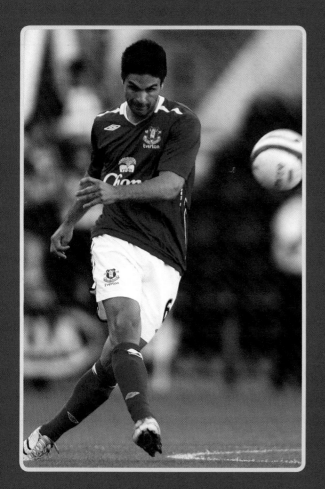

Nuno Valente

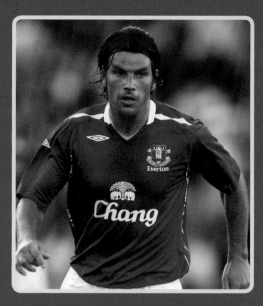

Nuno Valente arrived at Goodison Park from Porto days before the transfer window closed in August 2005.

An experienced defender who has represented his country on many occasions, Nuno was in the Portugal side which lost 1-0 to Greece in the Euro 2004 final.

A Champions League winner in 2004, he played under Jose Mourinho whilst at Estadio do Dragao and the Chelsea manager spoke to David Moyes ahead of his transfer highly recommending him.

Nuno's second season was blighted by injury and he barely featured after Christmas with a succession of niggling problems.

Patrick Boyle

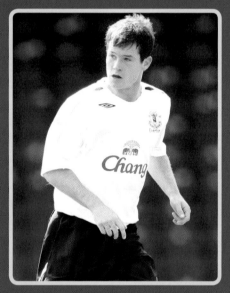

'Paddy' broke into the fringes of the first team after impressing in the reserves.

He attended the Everton Academy after coming to Merseyside from Glasgow.

Essentially a left back, he can also operate in midfield or in the centre of a back four.

His determined performances since joining the Toffees have also brought him Scotland Under-19 honours.

Paddy was named on the bench for the first time in the match at home to Chelsea in January 2006. The young Scot impressed in Everton's pre-season fixtures ahead of the 2006/07 campaign and was loaned to Norwich to gain experience.

He made three appearances for the Canaries but returned to Everton with a back injury. It was diagnosed as a stress fracture and Boyle was forced to sit out the action for the rest of the season as he recovered.

Phil Jagielka

Phil Jagielka joined Everton in the summer of 2007 from Sheffield United.

He arrived on Merseyside in early July in a deal worth 4m.

Rumours of a switch to Goodison Park had rumbled on all summer, and when Sheffield United's relegation was confirmed (following their challenge of the Premier League's decision not to dock West Ham points) the Toffees quickly tied up the deal.

Jagielka, who has England 'B' honours, is a versatile player.He can play in central defence, at full back and also in midfield.

He is also a capable goalkeeper and has been called into action for Sheffield United on several occasions, most notably when he kept a clean sheet in the Blades' 1-0 home win over Arsenal last season.

Jagielka was at Everton's academy for a period in his teens before progressing through the ranks at the Yorkshire side.

Phil Neville

England international Phil Neville arrived at Goodison in August 2005.

Renowned for his versatility, the younger of the two Neville brothers brought a wealth of European and international experience to Everton when he completed his transfer from Manchester United.

After collecting a plethora of medals at Old Trafford, Phil completed his switch down the East Lancs to Goodison.

A consummate professional, his signing was seen by many at Everton as further confirmation of the Club's ambition to maintain and build on the success achieved during the 2004/05 season.

He took over the Club captaincy at Goodison from David Weir when the Scotland international departed to join Rangers in January 2007.

Phil was one of Everton's most consistent performers during the 2006/07 season, despite playing much of it at right-back in place of the injured Tony Hibbert.

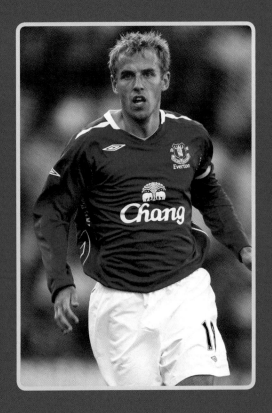

Steven Pienaar

Steven Pienaar is a skilful and dynamic midfielder.
He had played for some of the best teams in Europe before he joined the Toffees on loan last summer.

Steven grew up in South Africa, before moving to Holland where he emerged as one of the hottest talents in the game whilst playing for Ajax Amsterdam.

Before plying his trade in the Dutch league, he began his career at Ajax Cape Town - the satellite club of the Dutch side.

Steven excelled during his time at Ajax and was part of a very forward thinking side that contained Everton's Andy van der Meyde and Swedish star Zlatan Ibrahimovic.

Whilst in Holland he gained some vital European experience with Ajax's Champions League campaigns.

In January 2006, Borussia Dortmund secured the services of the South African on a three-year contract. Steven was signed as a direct replacement for the Arsenal-bound Tomas Rosicky and was also part of the South African squad at the 2002 World Cup.

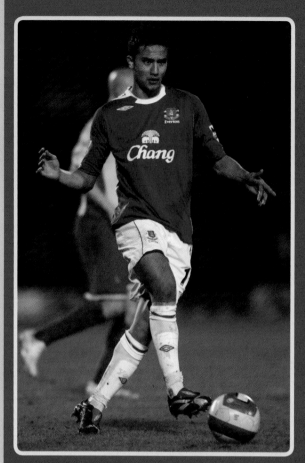

Tim Cahill

Sydney born Tim Cahill was David Moyes' second summer signing of the 2004/05 close season and the Australian has not looked back since his move from Millwall. A forceful, strong running midfielder, he is remarkably good in the air for a player of only average height. His first season in the Premiership saw him win the Player of the Season award at Goodison after finishing the campaign as top scorer.

He was, once again, a key figure for the side during the 2005/06 campaign. A knee injury sustained in April raised doubts about his availability for Australia in the World Cup but he was included in Guus Hiddink's squad for the tournament in Germany.

And he made a sensational World Cup appearance, coming on as a substitute in Australia's group game with Japan and scoring twice to turn a 1-0 deficit into an eventual 3-1 win.

Tim returned to Everton and began the season in sensational style, bagging seven goals before the end of October. He then injured his knee in a collision with Lee Carsley and didn't return until January 2007. His return was shortlived, playing six matches before breaking his foot in the 1-1 draw at Sheffield United in March 2007. During the summer of 2007 Tim returned from injury and put pen-to-paper on a five-year contract extension.

Tim Howard

Tim Howard joined Everton on a season-long loan in the summer of 2006.

He arrived from Manchester United, where he had fallen behind Edwin van der Sar in the goalkeeping pecking order.

Nonetheless, he made 77 appearances for United before agreeing the switch to Everton.

He began his career in his native USA, playing for the New York/New Jersey Metrostars, where he eventually replaced USA keeper Tony Meola as the first choice in goal.

He moved to Man Utd in 2003 and replaced Fabien Barthez. Three years later he arrived at Everton and gave consistently impressive performances in goal. Indeed, such was his impact that in February 2007 his move was made permanent.

In the summer of 2007, Tim collected his first piece of silverware since his move to Goodison.

The goalkeeper was an instrumental figure for the USA as they beat Mexico 2-1 to win the CONCACAF Gold Cup.

Tony Hibbert

Renowned by many as the best tackler at the Club, Academy graduate Tony Hibbert looks set to forge an impressive career with Everton.

Hibbert combines excellent defensive qualities with the ability to make intelligent forward runs.

Strong and not short of pace, his presence in the side provides a boost to the Blues' back four.

A member of the Toffees' 1998 FA Youth Cup winning side, Tony made his debut in March 2001 as Everton defeated West Ham 2-0 at Upton Park.

After a solid 2005/06 campaign, the following season started in disappointing fashion for Hibbert, as he was laid low with a rare tropical illness picked up whilst on holiday.

He did return briefly but then ruptured his groin and was out for three months. He made his comeback in the 0-0 draw at Anfield in February and played his part in helping the Blues secure a top six finish and a place in the UEFA Cup.

Victor Anichebe

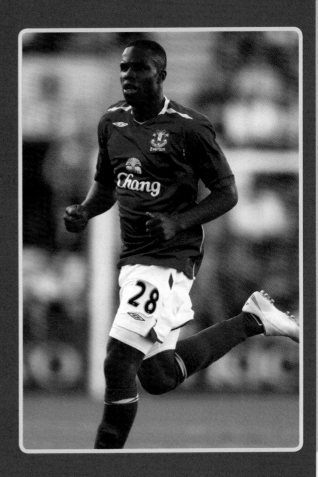

A powerful, fast striker, Victor was born in Nigeria but moved to Merseyside when he was three years old.

He progressed through the Everton youth system and became a regular Under-18 Academy player before graduating to the reserves.

He made his senior debut as a substitute in an FA Cup fourth round tie against Chelsea at Goodison in January 2006.

His first goal for the Club came on the final day of the same season, scoring in the 2-2 draw against West Brom after coming on as a late substitute.

Victor was named as the Reserve Player of the Year at the inaugural Club awards in May 2006.

The 2006/07 season saw him establish himself as a regular in the matchday squad, and he started three successive home games, scoring twice against Newcastle at Goodison Park.

Sylvester Stallone

Back in January, Everton welcomed a Hollywood legend to Goodison Park. Sylvester Stallone, better known as Rocky, was presented to the fans - and evertonTV was there to record an exclusive interview.

evertonTV

Keeping in touch with events at Goodison is now easier than ever - thanks to evertonTV.

The online channel is produced exclusively from Goodison Park and gives fans a unique insight into life within the Blues' squad.

Daily interviews from the manager and players, classic highlights of great Everton games from the past and extended highlights of every Premiership match are just some of the great benefits subscribers receive.

At the start of the 2007/08, a year after the launch of the web service, evertonTV was revamped and relaunched. The quality of the video clips improved, the site was made easier to navigate and more content from fans introduced – you could even be on evertonTV if you have been to Goodison Park this season!

If you want to get closer to the manager and players, then evertonTV is the only place to go. As well as unprecedented access to the training ground, providing behind-the-scenes footage and interviews, evertonTV also offers live commentary of every senior match, video clips from Academy and reserve matches and interviews with the stars of tomorrow.

The first ever TV interviews conducted by James Vaughan, Victor Anichebe and Lukas Jutkiewicz appeared on evertonTV – and it remains the place to see the stars of the future first.

A subscription to evertonTV costs just £4.99 a month or £40 a year. For details of how to take advantage of the service, visit evertonfc.com.

Season Review
part 2:

January

January was, in many ways, a surreal month for the Blues.

How else could you describe a month in which the team suffered a hammering at home in the cup, entertained a Hollywood living legend and managed to move up the Premiership table despite only securing one victory during the month.

It was also the month in which Manchester City showed something they failed to reproduce for months to follow - goalscoring form at home.

Unfortunately, it was the Blues on the receiving end. Two goals in the second half from substitute Georgios Samaras - including one penalty - consigned Everton to a New Year's Day defeat at Eastlands.

But it could have been very different. Leon Osman netted a late effort - and was then felled minutes later. Video replays revealed a penalty should have been given but, not for the first time during the season, the referee disagreed.

Nevertheless, Everton remained justifiably confident going into the FA Cup third round, despite the draw pitting them against Premiership rivals Blackburn at Goodison.

What followed, however, was the biggest defeat of the season for the Toffees.

Mark Hughes named a young side - but they managed to put the Blues on the back foot with Matt Derbyshire netting after just five minutes. By the time Andy Johnson pulled one back from the penalty spot with 20 minutes remaining the tie was already lost, with Henrik Pedersen and Paul Gallagher adding further first-half goals. Benni McCarthy made it 4-1 in stoppage time.

Disappointment turned to euphoria a week later when Sylvester Stallone arrived at Goodison as the special guest of Bill Kenwright. Stallone was in the UK promoting his film, Rocky Balboa.

He received a heroes welcome, but unfortunately Everton couldn't provide

Leon Osman keeps possession against Reading

him with a victory in their Premiership game against Reading, Andy Johnson netting to earn a 1-1 draw.

Despite only drawing that game, Everton moved up from eighth to seventh in the table.

And in the final game of the month they consolidated that position, Mikel Arteta scoring two at Wigan to earn a well-deserved three points.

The January transfer window also saw some activity at Goodison, with David Weir departing on a free transfer to sign for Rangers and Manuel Fernandes arriving from Benfica on loan.

Mark Hughes also left Goodison permanently, the reserve team skipper signing for Northampton.

Mikel Arteta converts his penalty at Wigan

February

February was the month the push for Europe began in earnest.

A trip to Anfield was one of the toughest away days for any side in the division. Liverpool found scoring at home no problem at all for the majority of the season - but not so when the Blues made the short trip across Stanley Park.

Tim Howard again showed his quality with an impressive performance - underlining why, just days later, he would sign a four year deal with the Blues after his loan from Manchester United was made permanent.

But Alan Stubbs was the real star of the show, producing a composed and inspired display in the heart of defence.

That point - making it four from Liverpool in the season - provided the springboard for a decent victory over Blackburn a week later. Making amends for the FA Cup exit, Andy Johnson netted the only goal of the game.

Tottenham broke Everton hearts 10 days later, the midweek match at Goodison going the way of the Londoners courtesy of Jermain Jenas' 89th minute strike. Mikel Arteta had equalised Dimitar Berbatov's opener with a superb free-kick early in the second half.

Spurs were in a rich vein of form at the time - and ultimately that late-late goal from Jenas denied Everton the fifth place finish they craved, with it going to Tottenham instead.

They were the two form sides in the table at that time, as the 3-0 rout of Watford three days later for the Blues illustrated.

Manuel Fernandes netted his first goal since his January arrival from Benfica on loan, with Leon Osman netting a cracker to add to Andy Johnson's early strike.

It was Everton at their vibrant best,

Alan Stubbs celebrates a clean sheet at Anfield

showing an eye for goal that helped them rack up a hugely impressive goal difference by the end of the campaign.

Phil Neville tracks back against Watford

March

Thanks to Everton's early exit from the FA Cup, coupled with international weekends there were just two matches to occupy the players in March.

Indeed, after the match with Sheffield United at Bramall Lane on March 3 there was just one game in a 28 day period for the Toffees.

But what a game it was! The victory over Arsenal was as pivotal to Everton's European qualification as the 1-0 win over Manchester United in 2005 was to securing a top four finish.

Andy Johnson, not for the first time, was the hero. He rifled the ball through a crowded penalty area in injury-time to send Evertonians into a state of delirium. Hail was falling on Goodison by that stage - but that merely added to the atmosphere.

Everton had deserved the win as well. There were a host of chances, the woodwork had been struck and Manuel Fernandes showed off his flair with a memorable cameo that left Arsenal's midfield in a spin.

By contrast, the 1-1 draw at Sheffield United was far less memorable. A Mikel Arteta penalty saved a point after Andy Johnson had been felled by Paddy Kenny.

But the Blues left Yorkshire disappointed, not least because influential midfielder Tim Cahill fractured his foot and was ruled out for the remainder of the season.

Having forged a strong understanding with Johnson in a 4-4-1-1 formation for much of the season, it left David Moyes having to reassess his options.

But the Arsenal victory showed there were plenty of other options in the squad.

Tim Howard and Andy Johnson celebrate the Arsenal win

Andy Johnson takes the ball around Paddy Kenny at Bramall Lane

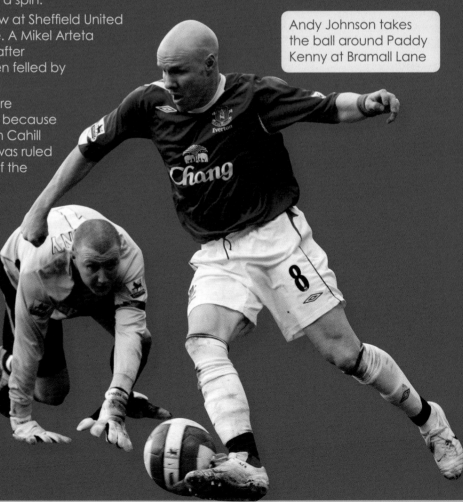

April

After the lull that was March came the storm of April - memorable victories, heart-breaking defeats and six matches in 26 days.

But the biggest news of April was the untimely death of Everton legend Alan Ball. One of the finest players to don the blue shirt - and one of the greatest to ever play the game in this country - died of a heart attack at his home in Hampshire.

Evertonians all over the world mourned his passing. The club opened a book of condolence that received thousands of entries and Alan's family were the guests of honour for the game against Manchester United at Goodison a few days later.

If only the match had ended as it should - with an Everton victory.

There was frustration after the first game of the month as well - an away trip to Aston Villa in which Joleon Lescott netted the first goal of his Everton career.

The former Wolves defender - a boyhood Villa fan - took great pleasure in netting the opening goal during an opening 45 minutes in which Everton played some of the most eye-catching football of the season.

James Vaughan, handed a shock start in the victory over Arsenal, continued in the side and caused countless problems for the Villa defence, whilst Mikel Arteta produced a couple of moments of real magic.

But a second half equaliser from Gabriel Agbonlahor with just seven minutes of the game remaining denied Everton the win their play merited.

There were no such worries a few days later, although Fulham took the early lead in the game at Goodison. Having never come from behind to win this season, there were fears it was going to be a night of frustration for the Blues.

Instead Lee Carsley, head bandaged, equalised and further goals flowed from Alan Stubbs, James Vaughan and Victor Anichebe to complete the rout.

A draw at fellow UEFA Cup contenders Bolton on the following Monday of the Bank Holiday weekend maintained the stalemate - and denied Everton the chance to move up to fifth and put fourth placed Arsenal under pressure.

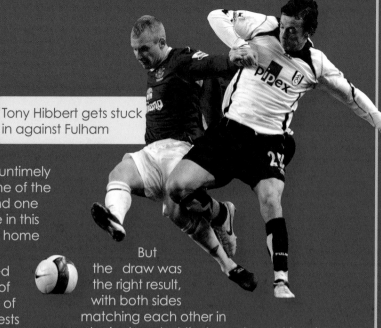

Tony Hibbert gets stuck in against Fulham

But the draw was the right result, with both sides matching each other in a physical contest that saw James Vaughan equalise for Everton before having to be stretchered off with a severed vein in his foot.

He missed the trip to West Ham as a result as Everton suffered a shock defeat that threatened to derail the UEFA Cup hopes.

Reading and Portsmouth were hot on Everton's heels and the Blues had tough fixtures remaining.

Manchester United were next up - and they arrived at Goodison desperate for the points to keep Chelsea at arm's length in the race for the title. Things started badly for them though.

Everton bossed the opening hour of the contest and fully deserved the 2-0 lead they took into the final third thanks to a thunderbolt from Alan Stubbs and an even better effort from Manuel Fernandes. Alan Ball would have been proud.

But then a slip-up from Iain Turner - in the side because of the ineligibility of Tim Howard - presented John O'Shea with a simple tap-in and the game turned dramatically. By the final whistle the Blues were 4-2 down and shell-shocked.

Joleon Lescott scores against Charlton Athletic

May

May was the decisive month for the Blues in their pursuit of a European place.

And when the side's mettle was tested, they delivered in emphatic fashion.

There were just two games to contend - but what games.

Portsmouth arrived at Goodison on May 5 knowing that a victory would have moved them above the Blues in the table - and pushed Everton out of the European places with just one game remaining.

Not surprisingly, there was a nervous start to proceedings, but David Moyes' men showed their edge in the second half, stepping up a gear after a goalless opening period to sweep aside Pompey.

Two goals in the space of a few minutes were the key. David Moyes had been bold with his team selection, starting James Vaughan and Victor Anichebe together in attack for the first time with Andy Johnson out with an ankle injury.

The young forwards, both still just 18, performed admirably and it was Vaughan who helped Mikel Arteta to open the scoring from the penalty spot - fouled by Glen Johnson as he charged into the Portsmouth penalty box.

Minutes later, Joseph Yobo powered a header from an Arteta centre past David James and the victory was assured. A late diving header from Gary Naysmith, his first of the season, sealed the points and, with Reading's shock defeat at home to Wigan, Everton were all but guaranteed a place in the top seven.

Only a record defeat on the final defeat to Chelsea would have jeopardised Everton's place in the UEFA Cup.

But the manager's focus was on winning that game - becoming the first manager

Joseph Yobo heads home against Portsmouth

to mastermind the defeat of Jose Mourinho at home in the league since his move to Stamford Bridge.

It would have also assured Everton of a fifth place finish. It looked as if the win was on course as well. Vaughan netted a well-taken opener as Everton took a grip of the game.

But a controversial equaliser from Didier Drogba denied Everton the three points and the fifth place Moyes coveted so much. The controversy surrounded a blatant foul on Mikel Arteta in the build-up to Chelsea's goal.

The referee allowed play to continue - and the Everton boss was banished to the stands for his remonstrations on the side of the pitch.

It speaks volumes for the progress made by Everton in recent seasons that a draw at Chelsea was regarded as a disappointment. Qualification for European competition for the second time in three years, however, more than made up for it.

Joleon Lescott joins in the celebrations

Ask your Dad

1   From which club did Everton sign Tim Cahill?

2   With which club did James Mcfadden begin his playing career?

3   Which Swedish winger signed for Everton from Arsenal in 1994?

4   Who scored a vital goal against Coventry in 1998 to keep Everton in top-flight football?

5   Who was made the first ever Everton manager in 1939?

6   Which 3 clubs did Everton face in FA Cup finals throughout the 1980's?

7   Who scored two goals in Everton's 1966 FA Cup final victory?

8   Who were the kit sponsors during Mike Walker's reign as Everton manager?

9   Who succeeded Harry Catterick as Everton manager in 1973?

10   Which club did Gary Lineker join when he left Everton?

11   In 1988, which striker joined Everton for a club record fee of £2.5 million?

12   Who scored the only goal in Everton's Charity Shield win against Blackburn in 1995?

13   Ray Wilson joined Everton from which club in 1964?

14   What four clubs has Alan Stubbs played for in his career?

15   How many goals did Duncan Ferguson score in his two spells at Everton - 49, 59 or 69?

Quiz Answers

International Blues

Joseph Yobo - Nigeria

Lee Carsley - Republic of Ireland

Tim Howard - USA

Nuno Valente - Portugal

Andrew Johnson - England

James McFadden - Scotland

Tim Cahill - Australia

Andy van der Meyde - Holland

Picture Quiz

1. West Ham
2. Phil Neville
3. Jens Lehmann
4. 28
5. Villa Park
6. Wigan and Sheffield United
7. Andrew Johnson, Olof Mellberg and Gareth Barry
8. Kevin Davies

Ask your Dad

1. Millwall
2. Motherwell
3. Anders Limpar
4. Gareth Farrelly
5. Theo Kelly
6. Liverpool, Watford, Manchester United.
7. Mike Trebilcock
8. NEC
9. Billy Bingham
10. Barcelona
11. Tony Cottee
12. Vinnie Samways.
13. Huddersfield Town
14. Bolton Wanderers, Celtic, Sunderland, Everton.
15. 59

Everton Quiz

1. Wigan
2. Sheffield United
3. 18
4. Andrew Johnson
5. Joleon Lescott
6. 5
7. 3
8. Bellefield
9. 60
10. Australia
11. James Vaughan
12. 1878
13. Paul Rideout
14. Villarreal
15. True

Spot the Difference